MY SOUL'S VERSES

JANUSHI RAICHURA

ISBN 979-888503519-4

I dedicate this book to my sister, who sparked my interest in poetry

Contents

Preface

Is God willing to prevent evil, but not able?
Then he is not omnipotent. Is he able, but not willing?
Then he is malevolent. Is he both able and
willing? Then whence cometh evil? Is he neither
able nor willing? Then why call him God?

~Epicurus

1. Divulging Facade

As I laid with my head on the pillow,
Staring at the fiery sun, and the beautiful willow,
With mugged up thoughts crammed inside my mind,
And Lucifer whispering at my side,
One after the other, fell my dreams like petals from a flower,
And the tears escaped the cage of my lashes, making my sweet
mouth sour.
Self-told words had now proven to be lies,
And the fake façade had come with a price.
No longer could I make believe,
No longer could I just live.
Bounds were unbreakable,
But my imagination had turned out to be killable.
And as it took its dying breath,
It planted one last seed in my head,
Told me it wasn't the boundaries,
The true Devil was the lies.
Imagination wasn't bound by any line,
It wasn't made to falsify.
I rose and fell,
Over the chime of a bell.
I had trouble standing,

But was it the costume I wore that led to my crash-landing?
Soon, the Angel reappeared at my shoulder,
And I felt a little less colder.
The realization hit, the illusion divulged,
The mask dropped,
And I saw my face,
Just as pretty, but no longer hidden behind a veil.

We often wonder why we are stuck someplace. Why we can't move forward. It's not that we are bound by some lines. Nor is it other people. It's us. It is the false pretence we put up to give a better impression of us.

Slowly, we start pretending that to our own selves. And how can you move ahead when you are lying to your own self?

2. Under The Sea

A lurch in my stomach was all I felt,

As I reached the world where countless wonders were held.

It was what I imagined flying,

I was scuba-diving.

The coral reef shone bright,

In the light of the blue sunlight.

I reached out to touch a fish

Whose skin felt nothing on my thick guise.

I dared to go a little deeper,

And it certainly grew creeper.

If the world emerged from the marine,

Then that was certainly where I wished for it to go back in.

The guide instructed us to go up,

In the sea, no time was enough.

The sea is a wild beauty. It's filled with mystery and is beyond imagination. Being in the sea has been the best experience of my life. It's impossible to describe the underwater beauty.

3. No Time

Living in towers with light,

But no time to see the flowers bright.

Sailing in copper boats,

But no time to make paper boats.

Staying under shower for long time,

But no time to see the streams shine.

Working in office all time,

But no time for a family dine.

All time online on internet,

But no time to catch the birds in net.

After becoming a grown up,

We don't have time to see the dawn sun.

Being secured from computer hackers,

But no time to play checkers.

Measuring angles all time,

But no time to see the sun shine.

We don't have time. We are all so hellbent on getting a life, that by the time we do, we have lost it. Life is not just about money or job. Life's about enjoying

those perfect little stolen moments between our work. Like breathing in the fresh air under the pink-tinted sky, staring at the dusk sun.

• 5 •

It's about being with people we love, doing things we love. Life is love.

4. Lonely

You all ask me,
'Who am I ?',
Not 'How am I?'.
You just see my face,
Not my hobbies.
With a tear in my eye,
I went to hear,
The chirp of my bird,
Who flew above me,
Ignoring me.
Today I realised,
I was lonely,
I am lonely,
But maybe I can change my future.
Hear everybody,
"You didn't reject me,
I rejected you.
You didn't make me lonely,
I made myself lonely.
You invited me to play at night,
But I stared at the shimmering stars bright.
And we'll see who will be,

how much successful in the future,
And at that time,
You'll all ask me how am I,
Not who am I."

5. Hope

Moon is like hope in the dark sky,
Beneath which, we all love to lie.
It gives us something to look forward to,
Emblazed in the night sky like a tattoo.
Fear, sorrow, horror, all bow to hope,
It is the one thing that helps us cope.
Hope gives love its definition,
Love gives hope its destination.
Like the moon, it disappears once in a while,
But it always comes back with a smile.
To hold on to hope,
Is to hold on to the rope,
That pulls us out of the darkness,
Out of the blackness.

Darkness. How do we imagine it? Everything black. And we have no idea what resides in the darkness. As a child we fear it, as a child, we are afraid of monsters and beasts that we believe to come with Darkness. But as we grow old, we *realize that no such thing as monsters and beasts exist and most of us lose our fear of Darkness. But if we feel clearly, there are beasts and monsters in Darkness. What is that chill we get sometimes when at night? The cold feeling? Our imagination? That is what we tell ourselves. And we cannot be more wrong. What does Darkness mean? Fear, horror, hopelessness, that is what is Darkness. All the bad things. If we see clearly, Darkness is everywhere, it is the Light that keeps it from us. Why do mostly all the bad things happen at night, and not in the light of sun? Because that is what Darkness is about. Even as grown-ups we sometimes face fear walking in the Darkness. It is because the feeling we get that makes us so afraid of it. So, I believe that beasts and monsters are bad emotions that reside in the Darkness. Why do we sleep at night and not in the day? Because facing the day is easier than facing whatever that is at night.*

When we compare moon with sun, we find a lot of difference. We know that moon reflects some of the sun's light that it receives. What is that some of the sun's light? Hope. It shows that Hope is most necessary in life, even more essential than love. Because until you know there is a reason to go on, you go on. In Darkness, we need hope above all. When we face Dark times, we need a Hope to keep going. Light, keeps Darkness from absorbing us into it. Imagine walking down a completely black passageway without the smallest amount of Light. What do you feel? Fear of tripping, falling. Hopeless of finding any Light near.

Everyone has to face night. The moon shows the amount of Hope that we have in darkness, failure. One day, the moon disappears and so does the Hope. But we know that the moon will come again. Even having the hope of having Hope in future, is enough to keep us going. And to keep going, we must not let the Light in our soul, the Hope, go away. We must hold on to them, and remember that once the Light is gone, it does not mean that it cannot come back. Though it is a little hard to light the fire and sometimes we might get some burns, in return it keeps every bit of Darkness away. It means that even though it is hard to hope for something when there is nothing to hope for, we must create some Hope for ourselves. We must find a way to bring Hope back into our lives.

6. Lovely

Lovely was the sun setting
Which I stopped having time to watch.
Lovely was my first barbie,
Which I threw after its leg broke.
Lovely was the chocolate milk,
Which now has lost its charm.
Lovely were the cartoon,
Which now seem like nonsense.
Lovely was trekking,
Which feels too easy now.
Lovely was dancing,
Which feels weird doing in public.
Lovely was that candy icecream,
Which seems too childish now,
Lovely was me,
Who now has changed.
Both for better,
And worse.

I have changed. We all have. Things stop mattering after a while or their meaning in our lives change. But we have new things in our life. Different things start mattering. After all, change is a part of life.

7. Void

There are times when I am ignored,
There are days when I am shunned.
My opinions are always neglected,
My existence is never attended.
I am invisible, unseen,
People love to pretend they don't notice.
Or maybe they don't, after all I am nothing,
I have been void on the inside and good girl on the out.
Hope has always been in reach.
But that is it.
The chasm in me just sucks emotions in,
Leaving me a miserable emotionless pit.

Sometimes, we all feel a little empty. Emotionless, or cold, upset.
We all came from void, and so, void resides in us. We just have
to be so full, that no void can suck it all in.

8. Glory

You know the glory of God,
Who is also known as Lord.

More beautiful than any princess,
Uglier than Crow.

More colourful than a rainbow,
Colourless like a tear.

Brighter than the sun,
Darker than a graveyard.

Sweeter than any candy,
Bitter than bitter melon.

Kinder than anybody else,
Horrifying than death.

You know the glory of God,
Who is also known as Lord.

Good with good,

Bad with bad.

What you do,
Will come back to you.

God is good to those who are good. But those who do wrong, face the wrath of the God. Like, he is beautiful, colorful, a source of light, sweet and kind to those who have spent their lives doing good. But he is ugly, colorless, dark, bitter and horrifying to all those who have debasted their lives.

9. Fates

They chose the yarn for my shroud,
Before I was even born.
They picked out the scissor to cut the thread,
Before I was even there.
One made the yarn,
One is weaving,
And one will choose my last breath.
They say the Fates are cruel,
That they are merciless.
But how can the one that has seen you all your life be cruel?
The ones that weave your destiny from your choices.
The ones that create you, knowing they'll be your destroyer.

There are known to be three Fates. One that

10. Hug Pillow

It tolerated my sweet kisses,
My bitter tears,
My tight hugs,
And all my stuff.
It has always been there,
It has never complained.
The pillow that I gave hugs
When I am filled with emotions.
I have thrown it in anger,
I have held on to it in fear.
I have given it an imaginary shoulder,
Which I cry on.
I have made it my best friend,
The only one that has been with me through my worst.

The Hues Of Samsara

My life was always different, even when I didn't know about it. But it supposedly changed after I had the worst headache of my life. And sometimes I wish the secrets were kept secret; for when revealed, they made everything a thousand times worse.

I exhaled, holding my head. I had the urge to bang my head against the wall, but I knew it would only make the pain worse. I was having crazy dreams, that lead to headache due to my best hobby; overthinking, and I had spent my whole afternoon searching for ways to deal with the headache. One thing about headaches: they are the worst. Had it been a stomachache or some type of body ache, I could just distract myself by watching TV or reading or studying or something. But with headache, it only made things worse; and it invited my worst demon: boredom to pounce at me. The pain was easier to deal with than boredom. Because when I am bored, I think, which causes more headache. I closed my eyes, trying to sleep but an image from my nightmare appeared. A little girl running on the roof of the apartments I lived in, and someone pushing her off, and she falling to death. I had this kind of dream before, when I was five. A baby thrown from the roof of a castle. I had an excellent memory when it came to dreams. Somehow, I remembered every detail; which surprised everyone but me.

I got up. I hated doing nothing. It was a waste of time, which I hated. I sat on my chair near my study table. My diary lay open in front of me. I grabbed a black marker from my pencil stand and started doodling on my arm. I drew two symbols: a crescent shaped moon behind the trapezium of my thumb, and a circle with a half circle and a plus symbol beneath it.

I had no idea where it came from, but I just felt the need to draw it. Over the years, I had learnt many things. Let me reframe it. Over the years, I have learnt everything possible. From drawing to singing to dancing to everything. Even some weird things like fencing and Latin and different symbols from different mythologies and looming.

The symbol felt familiar. I got up and took out another diary from my shelf: the one in which I note all the symbols I learn and their meanings. I flipped pages to the Alchemy section. It was filled with the symbols used by the Alchemists in the ancient times. I turned some pages until I saw the symbol. Beneath the symbol I had written: Pluto. For a careless moment, I thought it was nothing until, it hit me. It wasn't just the symbol of Pluto. It was also the symbol of death. Chills ran down my spine. I tried to convince myself it was a mere coincidence, but I couldn't. Because I knew, it wasn't. The reasons I studied different symbols was because I doodled them around; symbols whose meaning I knew not. And then I searched their meaning on the internet. Then, I started researching different symbols. I often had dreams about different symbols and languages. So, I started learning different languages too. I knew, three Indian, three Europe and an international language. I know how to write in Morse code and runes. And, I am thirteen. I am captain of two sports teams in my school and the class topper since kindergarten. I am what other mothers call, "Good example!"

I have friends, a lot of them. Best friends too. But I am a girl who loves shadows. That's where I stay. In the shadows. Apart from my achievements, people don't pay me much attention. Let me correct that sentence; Apart from my achievements, people didn't pay me much attention. But that was until I drew that symbol on my arm. Which changed everything, I stood for. I stood for someone who no one tangled with, because they knew better. I stood for the good quiet girl, no one paid much attention, I stood for revenge, the sweet taste of vengeance. For excellence. Now, I stand for forgiveness, for using silence as a voice not a way to hide in the shadows, for being noticed, for perfection, for precision, and above all, for being a hunter.

This is all present. I'll take you six months into the past. Back to the day, the moment, I drew that symbol; the symbol of the devourer, the end, the inevitable, or so I thought.

The symbol stood out on my pale white arm. And for once, I felt glad that I was having a headache, for I couldn't overthink about the symbol. At least not at that moment. I grabbed my purse and walked outside my room to my grandma's.

"Granny, can I go to the pharmacy? I couldn't find the medicine for my headache. I think I misplaced it somewhere."

"What's that symbol?" she questioned; worry lines deepening on her face.

"I just doodled it by mistake. It's nothing."

"It's not nothing. It's the symbol of death."

"How do you know that?"

"I have studied on that particular subject. But the 'how' is not important. The 'why' is important."

"I told you, I drew it by mistake. It was an involuntary action."

"You should be more careful. Drawing symbols like this: never ends well."

"What do you mean?"

"Go get the medicine you wanted. We'll talk later." I nodded, I knew better than to question her decision. I took the key of our house and close the door behind me as my grandma settled for her fifteen minutes evening beauty sleep. I walked below the early evening sky, sun blazing in front of my eyes. The pharmacy store was nearby. Right around the corner, as my dad said. I used my purse to block the sunlight and turned around the corner. As usual, a middle age man sat on the counter with a table lamp and few other medical stuff. The shop was covered with green wallpaper and the chemist was reading a newspaper. I had been there before twice, once with my grandma, and once with my brother Reyansh; but I had never noticed anything. At that time, I felt the urge to observe everything. The newspaper was of the previous day, I noted. Then mentally yelled at myself for that. I had bigger problems. Behind me, two men entered the shop. They looked like they were in their twenties and they were whispering something to each other. The chemist heard them and put down his newspaper. "How long have you been here? I am sorry if I didn't notice you."

"It's alright. I just got here."

"So, what do you want?"

"A little help. My head hurts, so I am sure what medicine I should take. I was thinking aspirin, but honestly, I am sure."

"I'll give you something mild." He said smiling. He rummaged around and came back with a box of tablets.

"Thank you." He removed his spectacles, and handed me the medicines. Reading lenses. I noted.

"Sir you want something?" he asked the men behind me. They turned to face him, their face mixed with anger and confusion.

"Excuse me?" one of them asked.

"He's asking if you want any help."

"No, we're fine." The other one replied, his eyebrows raised.

"Um...okay," I paid the chemist who was staring at me, in wonder and confusion.

"What's your name?" the first man asked.

"Grandma says not tell strangers my name."

"But we're not strangers, are we?" his accent turned thick and I realized something. That was the first time we talked in English. We weren't talking in Hindi before. Or Gujarati. We were talking in foreign languages. European. Spanish, French and Latin. In that perfect order.

"Do I know you?" I asked in English, trying to calm myself.

"It's a nice tattoo. I can sense death around you."

"I have to go." I spoke bluntly and ran outside the store. The strangers didn't follow. I unlocked my house as fast as I could and entered. I closed the door behind me. "Grandma! Grandma!" I called. No reply. I rushed to her room. She was sleeping peacefully on her bed. A little too peacefully. Death symbol. Negative thoughts rushed into my brain. I shook her. She didn't move. I pushed my thoughts aside and called her name several times. She didn't answer. I called my father, who was at work.

"Dad, it's nanny. She's not moving."

"Calm down, tell me more precisely, what happened?"

"Nanny was taking her nap and now she's not waking up!"

"Call the ambulance, I'll get there." I took out my nanny's phone and called the ambulance. A lady picked up the phone. I told her it was an emergency and told her my address. She told me the ambulance will arrive within half an hour, so i sat down to wait. By the time the ambulance came, i tried moving my nanny, but she didn't move. I had called my brother Reyansh who arrived just in time for the ambulance to come. They took my nanny's pulse, which i could've checked, but I was too afraid. Afraid to face the reality. My mom had died when i was young, so nanny took care of me; and now I didn't know if I could handle it if she died too.

• 27 •
VENTURES OF
GEM LAND
and the
Black Time
JANUSHI
RAICHURA

VENTURES OF
GEM LAND-2
The Gorgon's
Curse
JANUSHI
RAICHURA

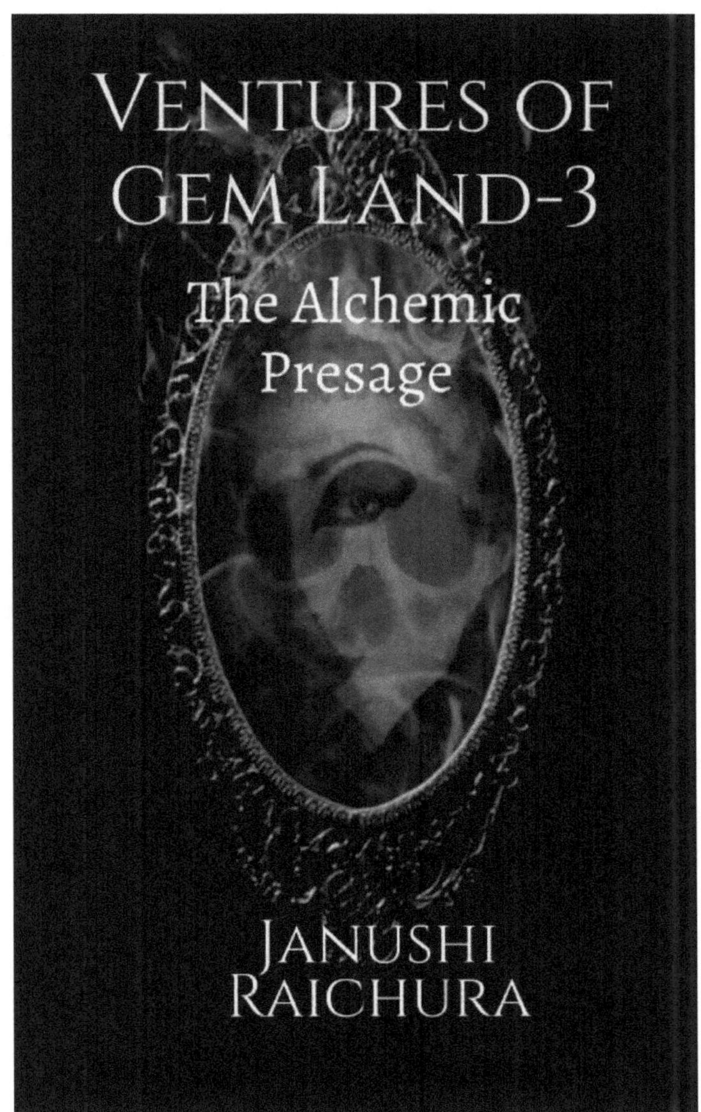

VENTURES OF
GEM LAND-3
The Alchemic
Presage
JANUSHI
RAICHURA

Janushi Raichura
WHO
THEE, MRS.
ANONYMOUS

VENTURES OF
GEM LAND

PART- 1, 2 AND 3

JANUSHI R